On The Line!
A Kid's Guide To The Royal Observatory, Greenwich, UK

Photography by John D. Weigand
Poetry by Penelope Dyan

Bellissima Publishing, LLC
Jamul, California
www.bellissimapublishing.com

Copyright © 2014 by Penny D. Weigand and John D. Weigand

All rights reserved. No part of this book may be
reproduced or transmitted in any form or by any means,
electronic or mechanical, including photocopying,
recording, or by any other means, or by any information or
storage retrieval system, without permission from the publisher.

The kids on the cover are from "Jan Van Egmond Lyceum" school, in Purmerend, The Netherlands.

ISBN 978-1-61477-133-3
First Edition

*All the world's a stage,
and all the men and women merely players;
they have their exits and their entrances;
and one man in his time plays many parts . . .*

William Shakespeare

Introduction

The Royal Observatory, Greenwich, UK is the home of Greenwich Mean Time and the Prime Meridian of the World. It is also home to London's only planetarium, the Harrison timekeepers and the UK's largest refracting telescope. If you are the scientific type, or if you are just interested in how time is measured and want to try your hand at some fun activities, there are lots of things to see and do at the Royal Observatory, a short and fun walk right up King William Walk. In the 'meantime,' set your watches!

See some of what photographer John D. Weigand saw through his camera lens, as you practice your reading skills through the use of word recognition, word repetition and rhyme The simple verse written by the award winning author, attorney and former teacher, Penelope Dyan, makes learning fun; and this book is a perfect starting point for parents and teachers to begin at to discuss the concepts of time and space. Author, Penelope Dyan believes learning should be fun; and these books are meant for kids, and they depict things that a kid would notice and want to see and to do. The photographs are original, and meant to stir the imagination and to get a child thinking. There is also a free music video on the Bellissimavideo YouTube Channel to further enhance the learning experience, for even more learning fun!

On The Line!
Bellissima Publishing, LLC

On The Line!
A Kid's Guide To The Royal Observatory, Greenwich, UK

Photography by John D. Weigand
Poetry by Penelope Dyan

You begin at King William Walk. You are looking for the line. Your mom tells you it's not too far, and you wonder what you will find.

You see a double line along the road.
That is NOT the line, you are told!

A squirrel runs down a line on a tree.
Now that is really something to see!

These walks and paths
make lines through the trees,
that serve as homes,
for the squirrels, birds and bees.
But none of these lines is the line
you are looking for,
and your mother says THAT line
does oh so much MORE!
You see, the line you seek
is NOT a path through the park.
The line YOU seek separates time,
and the daylight from the dark.

And then you arrive at the Royal Observatory.
You are standing right there!
You can't wait to look all around and see what's everywhere.
And one thing you really want to find, is that good old Prime Meridian Line!

And there it is,
measuring our world,
the place where measured time
was first excitedly unfurled.
You run and put one foot
on each side,
and your mom says laughingly,
"From time you cannot hide!"

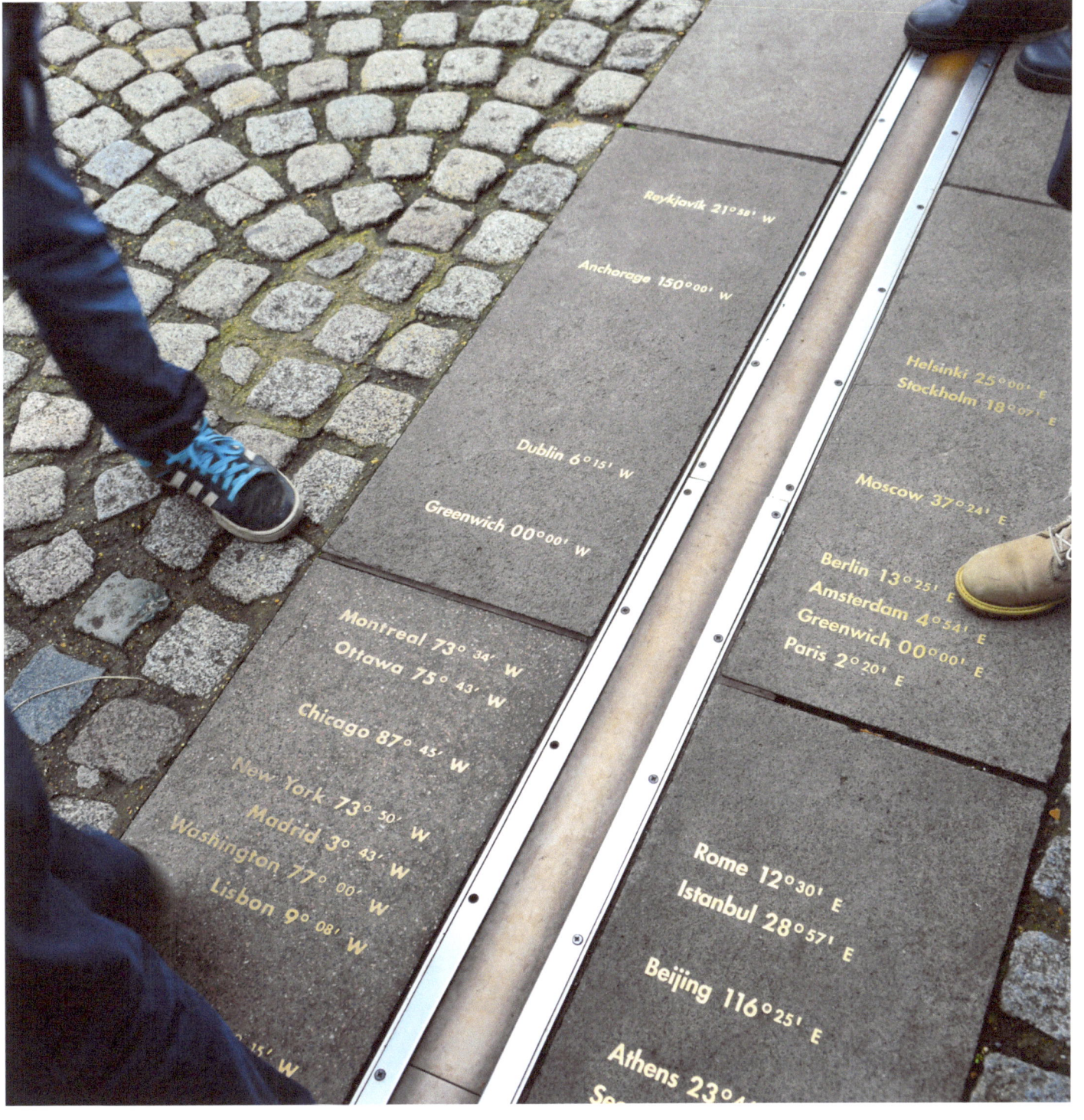

This is the place where men looked
up and into the sky,
and they measured the stars
that twinkled on high.
And they watched the magical
dance of time,
and discovered so many things
amazingly sublime.

And you imagine this figure
at the window is you.
And you think,
"If I lived in this place,
that is EXACTLY what I would do!
Yes, I would kneel upon a chair;
and through a telescope
I would stare!"

And I could watch these gears
that helped measure time and space.
I could do all of that
if ONLY I lived in THIS place!
And then as I watched
the moon rise higher and higher,
I'd wonder what inside of me,
the heavens might inspire,
as the gears opened up the roof,
and as I looked upward and aloof.

We go outside and look around,
to see what other things
might be found
There is a building called
the Astronomy Center,
and it's right next door too!
Mom says,
"There are activities inside,
that are simply
perfect for a kid like you!"

There is a rock in this place,
and the sign says it's the oldest
thing I will ever touch or see!
I wonder and I ask,
"How old could THAT possibly be?"
Mom also reads the sign;
and then I am told,
"This hunk of rock
is four and a half billion years old!"
And I notice if you look really closely,
that you can see a face!
It's staring right back at you,
from out of time and out of space!

Oh Yes! I do lots of very fun stuff,
and then we all go outside.
And from THIS view I cannot hide.
I see a house built for a queen,
one of the most magnificent
formal royal residences
that I have ever seen!
I wish that I could stay all day,
and in the grass below run and play.
I could pretend
I was in the 2012 Olympics, of course,
and ride upon a royal horse.
Because it was in that very year,
the Olympic equestrian event
was held right here!

"Today is the tomorrow
you worried about yesterday"

A Proverb

"Your yesterdays are the memories
you hold so dearly today."

Penelope Dyan

www.ingramcontent.com/pod-product-compliance
Ingram Content Group UK Ltd.
Pitfield, Milton Keynes, MK11 3LW, UK
UKHW060134240426
12048UKWH00002B/33